P9-DGV-704

MANIFEST DESTINY

THE
MEXICAN WAR

Borders drawn on maps meant little to
American pioneers pushing westward by
prairie schooner in the early 1840s.

MANIFEST DESTINY

THE
MEXICAN
WAR

ALDEN R. CARTER

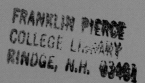
FRANKLIN PIERCE
COLLEGE LIBRARY
RINDGE, N.H. 03461

FRANKLIN WATTS
New York ★ Chicago ★ London ★ Toronto ★ Sydney
A First Book

ACKNOWLEDGMENTS

Many thanks to all who helped with *The Mexican War: Manifest Destiny*, particularly my editors, Reni Roxas and Lorna Greenberg; my mother, Hilda Carter Fletcher; and my friends Barbara Feinberg and Dean Markwardt. As always, my wife, Carol, deserves much of the credit.

Cover: With Congress debating a declaration of war against Mexico, the armies of American General Zachary Taylor and Mexican General Mariano Arista meet at Palo Alto on the Texas side of the Rio Grande River, May 8, 1846.

Maps by William J. Clipson

Cover photograph copyright ©: The Bettmann Archive

Photographs copyright ©: Historical Pictures Service, Chicago: pp. 2, 12, 19, 22, 32, 38, 50, 54, 57; Texas State Library, Photo Archives: p. 9 (photo by Eric Beggs); North Wind Picture Archives, Alfred, ME: pp. 10, 24, 30, 31, 42, 45, 47; New York Public Library, Picture Collection: pp. 14, 17, 20, 26, 34; Anne S.K. Brown, Military Collection, Brown University Library: p. 43; The Bettmann Archive: p. 52.

Library of Congress Cataloging-in-Publication Data

Carter, Alden R.
The Mexican War : manifest destiny / Alden R. Carter.
p.   cm.—(A First book)
Includes bibliographical references and index.
Summary: Discusses the causes, events, campaigns, personalities, and aftermath of the Mexican War.
ISBN 0-531-20081-7 (lib. bdg.) / ISBN 0-531-15656-7 (pbk.)
1. Mexican War, 1846–1848—Juvenile literature.   [1. Mexican War, 1846–1848.]   I. Title.   II. Series.
E404.C28   1992
973.6′2—dc20   92-10334 CIP AC

Copyright © 1992 by Alden R. Carter
All rights reserved
Printed in the United States of America
6 5 4 3 2

CONTENTS

**FOR THE
DAVE SHADIS FAMILY**

MANIFEST DESTINY

OFFICERS snapped commands. Sergeants bellowed. Troopers cursed as nervous mules and horses shied under the forgotten weight of packs and saddles. After seven months in the stifling heat and boredom of Corpus Christi, Texas, the army was on the move at last. The desert sun on March 8, 1846, found the lead cavalry units of General Zachary Taylor's small American army riding into the disputed borderland between Texas and Mexico. Ahead lay the Rio Grande River and a war that would change North America forever.

The land-hunger of the American people led to the Mexican War of 1846–48. In the 1840s, the United States was enjoying an era of spectacular growth as a flood of European immigrants swelled the population; new inventions revolutionized factory and farm production; and canals, steamboats, and railroads slashed distances. Settlers pushed west of the Mississippi River in ever increasing numbers, while explorers mapped routes across the Rocky Mountains into California.

As the nation prospered, more and more Americans imagined a future when the United States would stretch from Atlantic to Pacific oceans. "It is," a magazine editor wrote, "our manifest destiny to overspread the continent." Manifest Destiny became a slogan for all who believed that God, geography, and the energy, talent, and democratic values of the American people gave the United States an obvious right to the vast lands of the West.

Mexico held title to most of the territory lying in the path of Manifest Destiny. Mexico had won its independence from Spain in 1823, inheriting sparsely settled California, New Mexico, and Texas. Anxious to increase the population of these northern provinces, Mexico welcomed American settlers.

By 1830 American settlers in Texas outnumbered Mexican residents by three to one. Many of these new Texans refused to pay Mexican taxes or to obey the government's ban on slavery. Worried that Mexico was losing control of Texas, the Mexican dictator General Antonio López de Santa Anna (1794–1876) halted immigration and sent soldiers to enforce the laws. The Texans rebelled in the fall of 1835. The ruthless Santa Anna led a powerful army into Texas to smash the revolt. In San Antonio, he took no prisoners when his army overwhelmed 183 Texans defending an old Spanish mission called the Alamo. At nearby

Goliad, Mexican soldiers massacred nearly 400 surrendering Texans. Texans under General Sam Houston (1793–1863) struck back, crushing the Mexican army and capturing Santa Anna at the Battle of San Jacinto on April 21, 1836. To win his freedom, Santa Anna promised Texas independence as the Lone Star Republic.

At the Battle of San Jacinto, April 21, 1836, General Sam Houston's Texans overwhelm the army of the Mexican dictator, General Antonio López de Santa Anna.

BALING COTTON.

GINNING COTTON I

PICKING COTTON.

The labor of millions of black slaves
made the cotton-growing South rich
in the 1820s and 1830s. Northern
abolitionists bitterly opposed
opening up western lands to slavery.

Most Texans expected that the Lone Star Republic would soon become part of the United States. But the United States Congress hesitated. In the decades before the American Civil War, arguments over slavery divided Congress and the nation. The North based its prosperity on factories and small farms worked by free men, the South on the production of cotton grown by slaves on large plantations. Southerners wanted to push slavery and cotton-growing into the West. But a majority of Northerners wanted to halt the spread of slavery, and a vocal "abolitionist" minority wanted to abolish slavery entirely.

To hold the nation together, Congress worked out a series of agreements called compromises. New states were admitted to the Union in pairs, one slave and one free. In this way North and South maintained about the same number of seats in the Senate, where each state held two seats and each region could defend its interests. The proposed annexation of Texas threatened this delicate balance. Most Texans had strong Southern ties, and their vast land could easily be divided into several slave states. The added votes would give the South a majority in the Senate and a stranglehold on the government.

Northerners blocked the annexation of Texas for nearly a decade. Meanwhile, the Mexican government rejected Texas's claim of independence, and the area between the Rio Grande and the Nueces rivers became a bloody battleground. The fighting made the future of Texas a major issue in the American presidential election of 1844. Calling for the immediate annexation of Texas, Democrat James K. Polk (1795–1849) won a narrow victory. Polk's election weakened Northern opposition just enough for outgoing President John Tyler (1790–1862) to push an annexation bill through Congress. On his last night in the White House, Tyler offered Texas admission to the Union as a single state.

James Polk became the eleventh president of the United States on March 4, 1845. In his inaugural address, he warned other nations against challenging the annexation of Texas. His words were aimed not only at Mexico but also at

At pro-annexation rallies—like this one
in New York's Central Park—crowds clamored
to have Texas admitted to the Union.

America's great rival, Great Britain. Opposed to any growth of American territory, Britain was trying to arrange a settlement between Mexico and Texas that would keep the Lone Star Republic independent. Britain and the United States were also at odds over the Pacific Northwest. Both nations claimed what is today Oregon, Washington, Idaho, and southern British Columbia. Polk promised his audience that the United States would go to war rather than give an inch.

Polk meant only part of what he said. His actual plan—like the man himself—was more complicated. The new president was not a likable man. He was cold, crafty, humorless, and secretive. Yet he was also intelligent, efficient, and—despite poor health—worked extremely hard at his job. By fair means or foul, Polk intended to win American control of the Southwest and California. He soon let the British know that he would compromise on the Pacific Northwest in exchange for a free hand in dealing with Mexico. The British agreed to the deal.

Polk's tough talk outraged the fiercely proud Mexicans. Mexico sent more troops to the Rio Grande. Polk replied by sending a naval squadron to Galveston and ordering General Zachary Taylor (1784–1850) to gather an army in Louisiana. On July 4, 1845, the Texans voted overwhelmingly to accept annexation. Three weeks later, Taylor's army landed at Corpus Christi prepared for a showdown with the Mexicans.

President James K. Polk saw America's Manifest Destiny
leading westward to the shores of the Pacific Ocean.
When Mexico refused to sell California and the
Southwest, Polk found an excuse to use force.

With war threatening, Polk dispatched Congressman John Slidell to Mexico with an offer to settle the issue of Texas and to buy California and New Mexico. Polk's critics down through the years have argued that the president had no real interest in a peaceful settlement but hoped that his choice of the ambitious, Mexican-hating Slidell would doom the mission. It did.

Ignoring Mexican objections to his appointment, Slidell entered Mexico without permission on November 29, 1845. His unexpected arrival put President José Joaquín de Herrera in a terrible fix. In these years elections counted for little in Mexico as rival generals made and unmade presidents. Herrera himself had come to power late in 1844 when a revolt led by General Mariano Paredes had driven Santa Anna into exile. If Herrera even talked to Slidell, Paredes or some other general might push him from office.

Barred from any meeting with Herrera's government, Slidell stormed out of Mexico City on Christmas Eve, 1845. Paredes struck anyway, marching into the city a week later to take over the government. News of the snubbing of Slidell arrived in Washington, D.C., about the same time. By craft or accident, Polk had found an excuse to use force in the name of Texas and Manifest Destiny. He ordered General Taylor to advance to the Rio Grande.

OLD ROUGH
AND READY

Z A C H A R Y   T A Y L O R ' S little army arrived sunburned and footsore at the Rio Grande on March 28, 1846. The soldiers began building Fort Texas on the east bank of the river. On the far shore, Mexican soldiers in the town of Matamoros watched and wondered if there would soon be war. Taylor had no better idea than the Mexicans. His orders from President Polk cautioned him not to treat Mexico as an enemy. However, if Mexican soldiers made "any open act of hostility," he was to go on the offensive. Nearly forty years in the army had taught Taylor patience; he settled down to wait.

Taylor did not fit anyone's picture of a dashing general. At sixty-two, he was short, heavy, and homely. He shambled around camp in old shoes and a faded uniform without rank insignia. The common soldiers loved their homespun general. He looked after their needs, eased the harsh discipline of army life, and never ordered them to go where he would not lead. To them he was "Old Rough and Ready."

Taylor was confident that his men would perform well in battle. They numbered only 3,550, but they were the cream of the army: fast-marching infantry, heavily-armed cavalry called dragoons, and hard-hitting batteries of horse artillery. To lead them Taylor had a remarkable group of young officers trained at the United States Military Academy at West Point.

The Americans finished Fort Texas as Mexican rein-

Calm, fair, and tough, General Zachary Taylor
was called "Old Rough and Ready"
by his devoted soldiers.

forcements streamed into Matamoros and Mexican cavalry roamed the land to the north. The Mexican commander threatened war unless the Americans withdrew to the Nueces River. Taylor refused. On April 25, Mexican cavalry ambushed an American patrol, killing eleven dragoons. Taylor pulled in his remaining patrols and sent news of the fight to Washington.

President Polk received Taylor's report on May 9. With a treaty dividing the Pacific Northwest nearly complete, Polk no longer had to worry about war with Great Britain. On May 11, he asked Congress for a declaration of war on Mexico. After only the briefest debate, Congress voted overwhelmingly in favor. Polk signed the declaration on May 13, 1846. The formal beginning of the war made little difference to Taylor's men on the Rio Grande; they already had a fight on their hands.

Following the ambush, Mexican cavalry cut the road to Taylor's supply base at Point Isabel on the Gulf of Mexico, 30 miles (50 km) from Fort Texas. On May 1, Taylor left a strong garrison at Fort Texas and set out with the rest of the army for Point Isabel. His men spent four days resupplying on the Gulf, then turned about to fight their way back to the fort.

On May 8, Taylor's scouts discovered the Mexican army formed in two strong lines where the road passed a pond named Palo Alto. General Mariano Arista's men outnumbered Taylor's by more than two to one, but the Ameri-

In the first battle of the Mexican War,
American horse artillery routs Mexican
infantry at Palo Alto on May 8, 1846.

can horse artillery evened the odds. The batteries galloped
forward, swung their guns around, and poured a deadly
fire into the Mexican infantry. Calmly chewing tobacco,
Taylor sat sidesaddle on his horse, Old Whitey, as the guns
did their work. Arista threw his cavalry at the right end, or
flank, of the American line. Taylor's flank infantry regi-

ment shifted smoothly into a square and beat back the charge. Arista tried the left flank, failed, and gave up the fight for the day.

The next morning the Americans found Arista's army formed in a new line where the road crossed a dry lake bed called Resaca de la Palma. With the horse artillery laying down fire ahead, the American foot soldiers attacked through thickets of sharp, shoulder-high brush called chaparral. The chaparral turned the infantry fight into a confused brawl. Mexican cavalry hurtled down the road at the

In a headline charge, American cavalry overrun Mexican artillery at the Battle of Resaca de la Palma on May 9, 1846.

American cannons but were driven off by rounds of canister (tin cylinders filled with musket balls). American dragoons tried the same tactic but Mexican infantry threw them back. Taylor roared at the commander of one of his infantry regiments: "Take those guns and by God keep them!" The regiment's charge overran the Mexican cannons. The Mexican soldiers were brave but poorly led. The loss of the guns broke their spirit; they turned and ran.

Taylor's victorious little army reached Fort Texas that afternoon. Taylor was saddened to learn that the fort's commander, Major Jacob Brown, had been killed by a Mexican shell. He renamed the fort in honor of Brown. In later years, it would become the site of Brownsville, Texas.

The two battles had cost the Americans 34 killed and 113 wounded, the Mexicans ten or even twenty times as many. General Arista abandoned Matamoros and retreated west to the city of Monterrey. His report of the disaster on the Rio Grande threw the Mexican government into turmoil. President Paredes resigned in favor of his vice president. Soon after, General Antonio López de Santa Anna reappeared on the scene.

Santa Anna had been driven into exile by Paredes's revolt in the fall of 1844. From Cuba, Santa Anna sent messages to Polk, hinting that if restored to the Mexican presidency, he would sell California and New Mexico to the United States. Polk believed him just enough to order the American navy to let Santa Anna's ship sail un-

Summoned from exile to save Mexico,
General Antonio López de Santa Anna (center)
swore he would drive General Taylor's
army back across the Rio Grande.

challenged into the port of Veracruz on August 16, 1846. Many Mexicans disliked the strutting, luxury-loving general, but Santa Anna had energy, imagination, and great force of personality. With hope but not much joy, Mexico laid its fate in Santa Anna's hands. Giving up his plans—if he ever really had any—of making a deal with Polk, Santa Anna began raising a great army at San Luis Potosí to drive Taylor from Mexico.

In late July, Taylor's army had moved 100 miles (160 km) upriver from Matamoros to a new base at Camargo. Poorly sited in swampy ground, Camargo became a hellhole as thousands of ill-equipped, untrained, and disorderly recruits swarmed into camp. Disease swept through the army, killing some 1,500 men. The able-bodied were only too glad to escape when Taylor advanced on Monterrey in early September.

The Americans attacked the bristling defenses of the stone city on September 20. For three days they battered their way toward the city's central plaza. Finally, the Mexican commander, General Pedro de Ampudia, called for a cease-fire. After a day of truce talks, Ampudia agreed to march into the mountains while Taylor remained at Monterrey. Both generals hoped that their governments would make peace during the eight-week truce. They were disappointed.

President Polk had expected that a few American victories would bring the Mexicans begging for peace. Instead, the Mexicans had turned to Santa Anna and seemed more determined than ever. Polk decided that the Americans would have to threaten Mexico City itself to "conquer a peace." Too many rugged miles separated Taylor from Mexico's capital, so another army would have to be sent by sea. Polk ordered Taylor to hold Monterrey and nearby towns while his veteran infantry departed for the coast to join a new army under General Winfield Scott (1786–1866).

Santa Anna heard of the American plans and decided to try for a knockout against Taylor's weakened army. In early

January 1847, he left San Luis Potosí with an army of 20,000. Nearly 5,000 men died or deserted in the brutal 230-mile (370-km) march across a dry wilderness of mountains and deserts. On February 20, the army camped at La Encarnación, less than a day's march from Taylor's unsuspecting camp at Agua Nueva. No one in Santa Anna's

American troops batter their way toward the center of Monterrey, Mexico, during a three-day battle that nearly wrecked both armies.

exhausted army bothered to challenge a stranger in Mexican dress wandering through the camp. By dawn, Captain Ben McCulloch of the Texas Rangers had seen enough. He galloped north to warn Taylor.

Outnumbered three to one, the Americans fell back 15 miles (24 km) to a gorge just south of the Hacienda de Buena Vista. The next morning, Santa Anna found only smoking piles of abandoned American supplies at Agua Nueva. "They have fled," he shouted, and pushed his men forward without rest or water. That afternoon Santa Anna discovered Old Rough and Ready waiting at Buena Vista.

Few armies in history had suffered like Santa Anna's. Yet the Mexican soldiers attacked with desperate courage on the morning of February 23, 1847. They charged by the thousands up a narrow plateau between deep ravines. American cannons firing canister cut huge holes in their ranks, but the Mexicans kept coming. The American line began to collapse. Hurrying to the scene, Taylor was greeted by his second in command, General John E. Wool: "We are whipped, General." "That is for me to decide," Taylor snapped. Stripping the rest of his line to the bone, Taylor rushed every available man to the plateau and just managed to beat back the Mexican charge.

Mexican cavalry swept around the left end of the American line to encircle the army. Charging American dragoons and stiff fire from infantry in the hacienda buildings hurled them back. Mexican cavalry and light infantry

Outnumbered three to one, the
American army won a narrow victory in
the desperate Battle of Buena Vista.

broke through a soft spot in Taylor's line to the east of the plateau. Two American regiments—one commanded by future Confederate President Jefferson Davis (1808–89)—rushed to the spot. They formed a "V" with the open end facing the Mexican charge and slaughtered Santa Anna's soldiers. Santa Anna gathered his bleeding regiments and struck up the plateau again. Taylor turned calmly to one of his artillery officers, the future Confederate General Braxton Bragg: "Double shot your guns and give 'em hell, Bragg." Bragg did and the last Mexican attack broke.

It rained. Taylor's battered troops lay shivering through the night. Even their general doubted that they could hold off another Mexican onslaught. But the dawn found the valley beyond the ravines empty. Unable to get more from his exhausted men, Santa Anna had declared victory and led them south in the night. When the Mexican army finally staggered into San Luis Potosí after another cruel march, it numbered less than half its original strength. Santa Anna was no longer with it; he had ridden ahead to Mexico City in his luxury coach.

Zachary Taylor's war was over. He would remain in northern Mexico while others stormed the gates of Mexico City itself.

THREE

THE GOLDEN LAND

W H I L E Zachary Taylor's army marched and fought its way to Buena Vista, a struggle with all the twists of a spy novel was going on for the golden land along the Pacific coast of North America.

A century and a half ago, California was almost entirely wilderness. Some 9,000 Californios of Mexican and Spanish blood lived on the coast and in a few inland valleys. Los Angeles, with a population of 1,500, was the only town, all the other settlements little more than trading posts. Most of the 800 United States citizens and 400 settlers from other lands lived near Sutter's Fort in the Sacramento Valley. The people of California ranched, traded, and farmed with little interference from the government in far-off Mexico City. But the relaxed days in California could not last. American Manifest Destiny was about to arrive from several directions at nearly the same time.

In December 1845, the colorful explorer Captain John C. Frémont reached Sutter's Fort with sixty heavily armed mountain men, including the famous scout Kit Carson. In a slap at Mexican authorities, Frémont built a rough fort near Monterey and raised the American flag. The local military governor, General José Castro, promptly chased the troublemakers out of California.

Frémont was in Oregon, recovering from the embarrassment, when another impatient adventurer found him. Appointed a secret agent by President Polk, Marine Lieutenant Archibald Gillespie had crossed Mexico in disguise to reach Mazatlán, the base of the American naval squadron in the Pacific. After alerting Commodore John Sloat to the likelihood of war, Gillespie sailed north to Monterey. After more weeks of hard traveling, he found Frémont in early May, 1846. The two had no way of knowing if the United States and Mexico were at war yet, but they turned south to conquer California anyway.

Meanwhile, General Castro had made the mistake of cracking down on American settlers in northern California. A few dozen Americans from Sutter's Fort struck back in mid-June, capturing Sonoma north of San Francisco Bay and declaring the Bear Flag Republic. Frémont and Gillespie arrived, took charge, and marched on Monterey. The United States Navy got there ahead of them. Commodore Sloat had sailed north from Matzalán after hearing rumors that a British squadron was preparing to grab California if war broke out between the United States and Mexico. When Sloat anchored at Monterey on July 2, he heard news

Above: Card players receive a stern look from a priest
outside a California mission. The free-spirited
Californios lived peacefully alongside
Native Americans in a land of beauty and plenty.

Facing page: Soldier, explorer, national hero, and
relentless adventurer, Captain John C. Frémont set
out to steal California for the United States.

American settlers in Sonoma, California,
revolt against Mexican authority, declaring
the Bear Flag Republic on June 15, 1846.

of the Bear Flag Revolt and assumed that Frémont and
Gillespie were acting on orders from Washington. He im-
mediately occupied Monterey and put northern California
under the protection of the United States.

The aging and very proper Sloat was shocked to find
out a few days later that Frémont and Gillespie were acting

on their own. Fortunately for his peace of mind, his relief arrived soon after and Sloat was able to retire from the whole confusing business. Commodore Robert Stockton, Sloat's replacement, moved quickly to establish American authority over all of California. General Castro and Governor Pío Pico in Los Angeles tried to raise an army, but the Americans grabbed Santa Barbara, Los Angeles, San Pedro, and San Diego without difficulty. Castro and Pico fled.

Up to this point, everything about the conquest of California had been illegal. Finally, on August 17, 1846, Stockton received messages confirming that the United States and Mexico had been at war since May. He declared California a possession of the United States. That might have been the end of the story if Gillespie and Frémont had shown themselves a bit wiser and more trustworthy. As the new governor of Los Angeles, Gillespie was heavy-handed and insulting. The proud Californios revolted. Led by Captain José Flores, they drove the Americans from the town in late September. Stockton called on Frémont's tiny army at Sutter's Fort, but Frémont was too busy with other plans. Stockton scraped together a force of 400 men to retake Los Angeles, but Californios on horseback thoroughly outmaneuvered the American sailors and marines on foot at the Battle of San Pedro on October 8. A disgusted Stockton sailed for San Diego.

For the next two months, Stockton tried to find horses

for his men and Flores tried to find more fighters among the peaceable Californios. Meanwhile, a hard-bitten cavalry officer was crossing the deserts of New Mexico toward California. On the day war had been officially declared, President Polk had sent orders to General Stephen W. Kearny at Fort Leavenworth, Kansas. Kearny was to lead an army across New Mexico, capturing the major Mexican towns along his route, then cross the mountains to conquer California. Polk's orders demanded a march of 1,900 miles (3,100 km) through some of the harshest territory in North America. Fortunately, Kearny was just the man for the job.

The trading post built by Swiss immigrant John Sutter became the center of the thriving American community in the Sacramento Valley of California.

At fifty-two, Kearny probably knew frontier soldiering better than any officer in the army. Leading 1,600 regulars and volunteers, he set out for Santa Fe, New Mexico, in mid-June. The march across dry plains and mountains was the hardest part of the job. The people of New Mexico refused to fight for their unpopular Mexican governor. In return, Kearny treated them with courtesy. After occupying Santa Fe in late August, Kearny sent his Missouri volunteers south to join Zachary Taylor's army in northern Mexico.

The trek of the Missouri volunteers is an astounding story. Led by Colonel Alexander Doniphan, the 856 Missourians and their civilian train of more than 300 wagons crossed 2,500 miles (4,000 km) of rugged country. Along the way, they handily defeated far stronger Mexican armies near El Paso, Texas, and Chihuahua, Mexico. Yet, when they finally rolled into Taylor's camp on May 21, 1847, they had lost only a handful of men. Told that there was no more fighting to do in northern Mexico, the Missourians rested a few days, then set out for home.

Kearny had completed his own long march months before. Soon after leaving Santa Fe, he was met by Kit Carson, who carried an out-of-date letter from Stockton stating that all was peaceful in California. Kearny sent most of his soldiers back to Santa Fe and led 100 dragoons across the mountains into California. Only then did he learn of the renewed fighting.

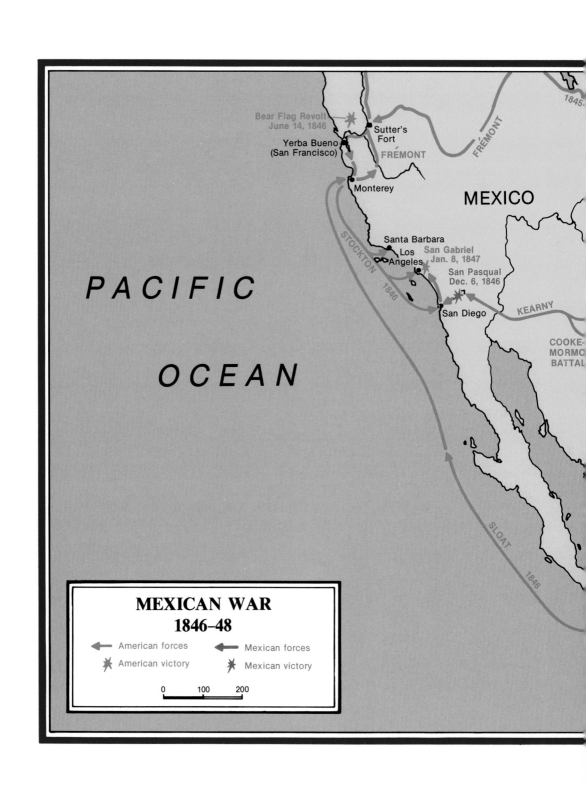

Bear Flag Revolt
June 14, 1846

Sutter's
Fort

Yerba Bueno
(San Francisco)

FRÉMONT

FRÉMONT

1845–

Monterey

MEXICO

PACIFIC

Santa Barbara
Los
Angeles

San Gabriel
Jan. 8, 1847

San Pasqual
Dec. 6, 1846

STOCKTON

1846

OCEAN

San Diego

KEARNY

COOKE-
MORMO
BATTAL

SLOAT

1846

MEXICAN WAR
1846–48

←— American forces ←— Mexican forces

✹ American victory ✹ Mexican victory

0   100   200

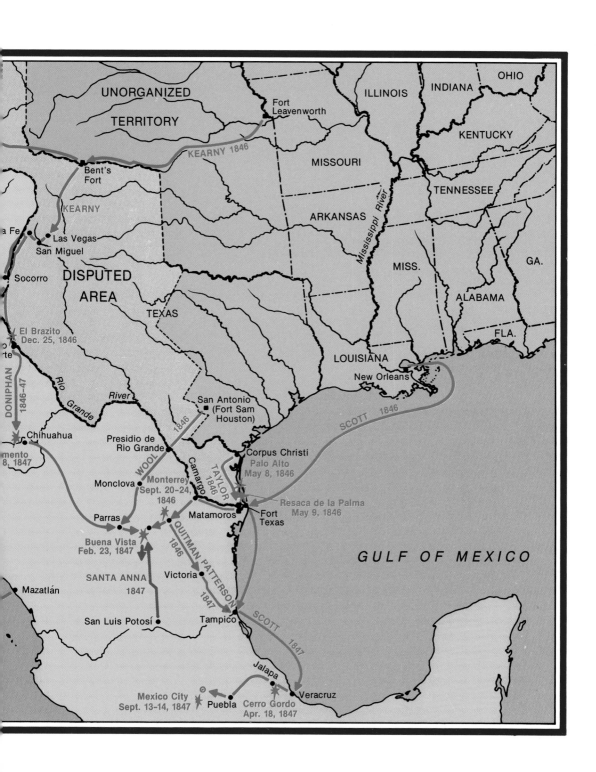

UNORGANIZED
TERRITORY

Fort
Leavenworth

ILLINOIS

INDIANA

OHIO

KEARNY 1846

MISSOURI

KENTUCKY

Bent's
Fort

KEARNY

TENNESSEE

ARKANSAS

a Fe

Las Vegas
San Miguel

Mississippi River

Socorro

DISPUTED
AREA

MISS.

GA.

ALABAMA

TEXAS

El Brazito
Dec. 25, 1846

FLA.

te

DONIPHAN
1846-47

Rio

Grande

River

LOUISIANA

New Orleans

San Antonio
(Fort Sam
Houston)

1846

Chihuahua

WOOL

Presidio de
Rio Grande

Corpus Christi
Palo Alto
May 8, 1846

SCOTT   1846

mento
8, 1847

Monclova

Monterrey
Sept. 20-24,
1846

Camargo

TAYLOR
1846

Parras

Buena Vista
Feb. 23, 1847

QUITMAN

1846

PATTERSON

Matamoros

Fort
Texas

Resaca de la Palma
May 9, 1846

GULF   OF   MEXICO

SANTA ANNA
1847

Victoria

Mazatlán

1847

San Luis Potosí

Tampico

SCOTT   1847

Jalapa

Mexico City
Sept. 13-14, 1847

Puebla

Cerro Gordo
Apr. 18, 1847

Veracruz

Less than 40 miles (65 km) from the safety of Stockton's base at San Diego, Kearny's exhausted troopers were attacked by Californio cavalry on December 6, 1846. Nearly a third of the Americans were killed or wounded and the rest surrounded. Carson and several other volunteers managed to crawl through the Californio lines to find help. Sailors and marines hurried from San Diego, and the Californios galloped away.

In San Diego, Kearny trained Stockton's sailors and marines for fighting ashore. Late in December, the Americans marched north toward Los Angeles. Captain Flores had done his best to keep the Californio revolt alive, but he could find neither the men nor the cannons to stand against the Americans. Two small battles later, Flores fled to Mexico and the Americans camped outside Los Angeles.

On January 14, 1847, Frémont strutted into camp. Absent all the time he might have done Kearny and Stockton some real good, he presented the astonished officers with a peace treaty signed by the brother of the former Mexican governor, Pío Pico. Centuries of Spanish and Mexican rule had ended in the golden land of California. The United States stretched from coast to coast at last.

Facing page: In Santa Fe, General Stephen Kearny reads the proclamation making New Mexico part of the United States.

FUSS AND FEATHERS

F R O M his height of six feet five inches, General Winfield Scott looked down on most people, particularly politicians. Not yet sixty, Scott had been a general for over thirty years and general-in-chief of the United States Army for six. Proud, blunt, and brilliant, he made little secret of his presidential ambitions. President Polk hated him.

Early in the war Polk tried to push Scott aside, but by the fall of 1846, he needed Scott. The war was losing popularity rapidly as American losses mounted and the Mexicans stubbornly refused to make peace. Some of America's leading writers and thinkers spoke out against the war. In Concord, Massachusetts, the philosopher Henry David Thoreau (1817–1862) spent a night in jail rather than pay a tax of one dollar to a government that he thought was doing evil.

Many Northerners believed that the war was nothing

more than a huge land-grab by Southern cotton interests. Antislavery members of Congress, including former president John Quincy Adams (1767–1848), tried to cut off funding for the war. When this failed, they tried to pass the Wilmot Proviso forbidding slavery in any territory gained in the war. Southern senators killed the Proviso after one of the angriest debates in the history of the Senate.

With Congress and the American people running out of patience, Polk swallowed his pride and approved Scott's plan to land an army on the east coast of Mexico for an overland strike at Mexico City. Scott threw himself into the task of gathering a fleet of ships and landing craft, a mountain of supplies, and thousands of wagons, horses, mules, and men. Soldiers more comfortable with the rough-and-ready ways of Zachary Taylor complained about the parade-ground strictness of "Old Fuss and Feathers" Scott. Yet Scott was a master of military organization and, as he would soon prove, a daring battlefield commander.

On March 9, 1847, Scott's men stormed ashore just south of the port of Veracruz, Mexico. They set up batteries of heavy cannons to shell the crowded city into surrender. The guns opened fire on the evening of March 22, turning the streets of Veracruz into a hell of shrieking shell fragments and tumbling bricks. After three days, the Mexican commander gave up the fight.

Scott established his supply base at Veracruz and pre-

Above: The American army lands at Mexico's
Gulf coast port of Veracruz on March 9, 1847.

Facing page: A small crowd listens eagerly to the
latest news of the fighting in Mexico, as shown
in this well-known nineteenth-century painting.

pared to move inland. His 8,500 soldiers faced a march of some 300 miles (500 km) from the tropical lowlands around Veracruz, over mountains and desert highlands, to the fabled Valley of Mexico and the ancient capital of Mexico City. They also faced the anger of the Mexican people and their sometime leader General Antonio López de Santa Anna.

While Scott's men were landing at Veracruz, Santa Anna's starving soldiers were stumbling south from Buena Vista. Santa Anna abandoned his army to hurry to Mexico City. His claim of victory over Zachary Taylor quieted discontent in the capital, and Santa Anna set about gathering another army to defeat Scott on the road from Veracruz.

Santa Anna's 12,000 men made a stand at the mountain pass of Cerro Gordo, 62 miles (100 km) west of Veracruz. Mexican cannons on three high hills commanded the road. To the right a river gorge cut off any path for an American attack. Santa Anna judged the steep, brush-filled gullies to the left equally impassable. But Captain Robert E. Lee (1807–1870), Scott's acting chief engineer, found a way. Following a narrow trail cut by Lee's engineers, an American division edged around Santa Anna's left flank to get behind the Mexican guns. On the morning of April 18, the Americans came roaring out of the gullies. The Mexican army shattered under the blow. Santa Anna threw away his fancy uniform and fled on foot.

General Winfield Scott salutes
cheering soldiers after the Battle
of Cerro Gordo on April 18, 1847.

The American army marched onto the high Mexican Plateau. Every mile added to Scott's supply problems, as Mexican raiders destroyed bridges and cut up his convoys from Veracruz. At Puebla, two-thirds of the way to Mexico City, Scott halted for three frustrating months while supplies and reinforcements caught up. Finally, with 11,000 men in four divisions, he cut his supply line to Veracruz and began the final march on Mexico City.

During the lull, Santa Anna had raised a new army. With 30,000 men, he waited for Scott to come down into the Valley of Mexico. On August 10, American soldiers paused in awe as they came over the high ridge at the base of 17,887-foot (5,450-m) Mount Popocatépetl and saw the Valley of Mexico spread out below. Twenty-five miles (40 km) away, in the center of a flat, green plain, stood Mexico City.

From that distance the march looked easy, but the plain was dotted with lakes, swamps, and barren fields of lava. Santa Anna barred the main highway, forcing Scott to detour along back roads. On August 18, Scott's army reached the village of San Agustín eight miles (13 km) south of the city, only to find the way blocked by 20,000 Mexicans holding a strong line along the Churubusco River. Lee found a trail to the west across a lava field called the Pedregal. Scott boldly split his army, holding one half on the road running north and sending the other half

Mexico City, capital and
heart of a proud nation

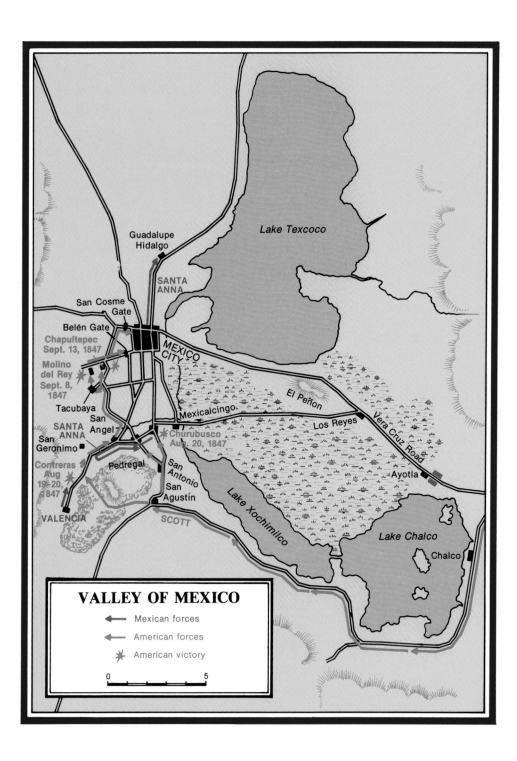

Lake Texcoco

Guadalupe
Hidalgo

SANTA
ANNA

San Cosme
Gate

Belén Gate

Chapultepec
Sept. 13, 1847

Molino
del Rey
Sept. 8,
1847

MEXICO
CITY

El Peñon

Tacubaya

SANTA
ANNA

San
Angel

Mexicalcingo

Los Reyes

Vera Cruz Road

San
Geronimo

Churubusco
Aug. 20, 1847

Contreras
Aug
19-20,
1847

Pedregal

San
Antonio
San
Agustín

Ayotla

VALENCIA

SCOTT

Lake Xochimilco

Lake Chalco

Chalco

VALLEY OF MEXICO

← Mexican forces

← American forces

✳ American victory

0   5

across the Pedregal to surprise the far right end of Santa Anna's line.

Meanwhile, one of Santa Anna's rivals, General Gabriel Valencia, made a bid for glory by advancing 4 miles (6.5 km) south of his assigned position at the right end of the Mexican line. Crossing the Pedregal, Scott's lead division stumbled on Valencia's 5,000 veterans near the village of Contreras early in the afternoon of August 19. The unexpected battle gave Santa Anna his great chance. He came pounding down the road from the north with his main force. Caught between two larger forces, the Americans hardly had a chance. But then Santa Anna lost interest in saving his political rival and turned around without attacking.

Hardly believing their luck, the Americans regrouped. On the morning of August 20, they smashed into Valencia's camp, driving his disheartened soldiers north toward the Churubusco. On the east side of the Pedregal, another American division roared up the road from San Agustín toward the river. As the Mexican line collapsed, Santa Anna ordered the bridge at the village of Churubusco held at all costs. His veterans rallied as the Americans poured into the town. It took Scott's men four bloody hours to take the bridge.

At the cost of 1,000 casualties, the Americans had won a spectacular victory: killing, wounding, or capturing some 7,000 of Santa Anna's soldiers and scattering the

American soldiers storm Mexican fortifications
at the Battle of Churubusco on August 20, 1847.

rest. Mexico City lay at Scott's mercy. Santa Anna asked for a truce. Scott, who hoped to avoid more bloodshed, agreed. It was a mistake. Instead of negotiating a peace, Santa Anna used the truce to rally his army. He put his men to work strengthening the outlying forts and fortifying the stone causeways that bridged the swampy land around the city. By the time Scott lost patience on September 7, the city was no longer an easy target.

On September 8, the Americans attacked Molino del Rey, a one-time flour mill fortified to protect the southwestern approaches to the city. What was supposed to be a minor action turned into a vicious slugging match. American skill and artillery won again, but the fight cost Scott's army another 116 dead and 671 wounded. Alone in the middle of a hostile country, the army was bleeding to death with every victory. Scott knew that his army no longer had the strength to fight its way back to the coast; the Americans must break down the gates of Mexico City or die in the attempt.

The great palace of Chapultepec barred the way. The summer residence of the president of Mexico stood atop a 200-foot (60-m) hill that had been a retreat for the nation's rulers since the Montezuma kings of Aztec Mexico. The palace's guns commanded the mouth of two causeways leading into the city. Perhaps more important, the palace symbolized the ancient honor and glory of Mexico; its fall would break both the defense and the heart of the capital.

American gunners hurl shot into
the Mexican fortress of Molino
del Rey on September 8, 1847.

All through September 12, American cannoneers tried to hammer Chapultepec into surrender, but the Mexicans held stubbornly to the "Halls of Montezuma." General Nicolás Bravo, an aging hero of the Mexican Revolution, steadied his 1,000 men. Among them were about 50 military cadets, some as young as thirteen. Bravo tried to send the boys to safety, but they refused to leave. Night fell and gloom settled on the Americans as they prepared to storm the high walls of the palace. General William Worth, Scott's second in command, told a friend, "We shall be defeated." Even Scott admitted to "misgivings" about the attack.

The American cannons resumed firing at dawn. At 7:30 A.M. they stopped, and for a brief moment, the morning seemed to stand still. Then with a shout, the Americans charged Chapultepec from three sides. The American cannons opened up again, spraying the park and walls in front of the advancing Americans. The Mexicans gave ground foot by stubborn foot. At the walls, the first wave of Americans crouched for fifteen agonizing minutes waiting for reinforcements. The second wave hit the walls with dozens of ladders, and the Americans scrambled over with swords and bayonets swinging. The Mexicans fought like demons, but the flood of Americans drove them back through the palace halls. At least half a dozen of the cadets died in the fighting. Legend says that rather than surrender,

one of them wrapped himself in the Mexican flag and leaped from the walls to his death.

As the Stars and Stripes rose over the towers of Chapultepec, two American divisions raced up the causeways toward the city gates. The Mexicans fought back at every turn and house along the way. At dusk General Worth's division finally broke through the San Cosme gate into the city itself. That night the remains of Santa Anna's last army retreated to the town of Guadalupe Hidalgo. Mexico City surrendered the next morning.

An American officer leads
his men over the walls of
the palace of Chapultepec
on September 13, 1847.

TRIUMPH AND TRAGEDY

S C O T T ' S ragged, battle-weary army occupied Mexico City on September 14, 1847. Santa Anna resigned the presidency, and a new Mexican government opened peace talks with the Americans. In early January 1848, Mexico agreed to give up all claims to Texas, California, and the Southwest in exchange for $15 million and another $3.25 million in forgiven debts. The United States gained what would become the states of Texas, California, Nevada, Utah, Arizona, New Mexico, and parts of Wyoming and Colorado.

The treaty of Guadalupe Hidalgo became official on May 25, 1848. The last American soldiers left Mexico the following July. Always outnumbered, they had won every major battle. But they had paid a price: no American armies before or since suffered a higher percentage of losses. Some 1,700 soldiers died in battle, another 12,000 of disease, accidents, or lingering wounds. Mexican losses were at least several times higher.

Unfair criticism of Winfield Scott's handling of the campaign derailed his political plans. Instead, Zachary Taylor became the Whig candidate for president in 1848, handily defeating Polk's ally Senator Lewis Cass. An exhausted and disappointed Polk died three months after leaving office. Poorly prepared for the presidency, Taylor

General Winfield Scott enters Mexico City on September 14, 1847. The peace Scott's victory forced on Mexico would embitter relations between the two nations for more than a century.

failed to unite a country splitting over the division of the West into slave and free states. He died sixteen months into his term and was followed by weak presidents who did no better. In the spring of 1861, the American Civil War tore apart the nation.

Still general-in-chief, Winfield Scott directed the Northern armies for the first year of the war until age and politics forced him to retire. More than 200 of the junior officers who had served in Mexico became generals in America's most tragic war. Robert E. Lee's skill and daring won astounding victories for the Confederacy. But Ulysses S. Grant (1822–1885), a little-known veteran of Scott's campaign in Mexico, rallied the Union armies and led them to final victory in 1865.

In the decades following the Civil War, the United States used the wealth of the lands won from Mexico to become a world superpower. Deprived of a third of its territory, Mexico suffered generations of poverty and unrest. Mexico never forgot its painful defeat, but the frightful bloodshed of the Civil War largely washed away America's memory of the Mexican War. A convenient forgetfulness also played a part. America has never been comfortable in recalling its triumph over Mexico. Patient negotiation probably could have resolved the issue of Texas, but President Polk and a willing Congress chose war instead. The United States had achieved its Manifest Destiny, but at what price to the American conscience?

In his *Memoirs*, Ulysses S. Grant called the Mexican War "the most unjust war ever waged by a stronger against a weaker nation." Yet Grant chose to serve despite his moral misgivings. Henry David Thoreau spent his night in jail musing on the responsibility of the individual to oppose unjust actions of government. He stated his arguments for peaceful protest in the famous essay "Civil Disobedience," a work that would influence Mahatma Gandhi, Martin Luther King, Jr., and millions of others worldwide.

Today some 55 million people of many cultures live in the lands the United States won from Mexico. South of the border, 100 million Mexicans are striving to strengthen their democracy and to raise their nation's standard of living. Despite shared interests in drug control, immigration policy, economic development, and environmental protection, bitterness and distrust still plague the relationship between the "distant neighbors." The future well-being of this continent depends on finding ways to reach across a century and a half of differences with friendship and understanding.

SUGGESTED READING

Carter, Alden R. *Last Stand at the Alamo*. New York: Franklin Watts, 1990.

_____. *The Civil War*. New York: Franklin Watts, 1992.

Chidsey, Donald. *The War with Mexico*. New York: Crown, 1968.

Downey, Fairfax. *Texas and the War with Mexico*. New York: American Heritage, 1961.

Eisenhower, John S. D. *So Far from God: The U.S. War with Mexico 1846–1848*. New York: Random House, 1989.

Nevin, David. *The Mexican War*. Alexandria, Va.: Time-Life, 1978.

Nichols, Edward. *Zach Taylor's Little Army*. New York: Doubleday, 1963.

INDEX